WIDE WORLD

# PEOPLE *of the* GRASSLANDS

David Lambert

WAYLAND

People *of the* **GRASSLANDS**
People *of the* **DESERTS**
People *of the* **ISLANDS**
People *of the* **MOUNTAINS**
People *of the* **POLAR REGIONS**
People *of the* **RAIN FORESTS**

**Cover:** Vaqueiros (cowboys) on a cattle ranch in Saõ Paulo, Brazil.

**Title page:** A family of herders with their yurt on the steppes of China.

**This page and Contents page:** Two combine harvesters in a field of wheat in the North American prairies.

Consultant: Anne Marley, Principal Librarian, Children and Schools Library Service, Hampshire.
Series editor: Polly Goodman
Book editor: Jen Green
Series and book designer: Joyce Chester

First published in 1997 by
Wayland Publishers Ltd
61 Western Road, Hove
East Sussex, BN3 1JD, England



Find Wayland on the Internet at
http: / /www.wayland.co.uk

**British Library Cataloguing in Publication Data**
Lambert, David, 1932–
People of the Grasslands. – (Wide World)
1. Grasslands – Juvenile literature
2. Human ecology – Juvenile literature
I.Title
305.8'009153

ISBN 0 7502 2012 0

Typeset in England by Joyce Chester.
Printed and bound by Eurografica, Italy

# Contents

# *Grassland People*

What do a park ranger in Tanzania, a wheat farmer in Canada, a cattle rancher in Argentina and a horse herder in Mongolia have in common? They all live on the vast, open plains that are the world's grasslands. Grasslands cover huge areas of every continent except Antarctica. Wild grasslands are home not just to people, but to a huge variety of animals and plants.

## Flimsy but tough

Wild grasses are small, flimsy plants compared to trees. Cattle, antelopes, sheep and rabbits can nibble grass leaves and stems right down to the ground. Hot sun can shrivel grasses, and floods can drown them. Fires can burn them to ash. Yet grass is tougher than it looks. Underground grass stems or seeds survive almost any disaster and still put out new shoots.

A gaucho (cowboy) ▶ rides across a treeless plain in Argentina. There used to be many more cowboys tending great herds of cattle in both South and North America.

## Food for all

It is lucky for us that grass plants are tough, because we depend upon them for our most important foods. Bread and breakfast cereals come mostly from the seeds of wheat or maize, which are two types of cultivated grass. Rice is also a type of grass seed. More than half the world's sugar today is from the juice from the stems of the tall grass, sugar-cane. Meat, milk, cheese and butter come from animals including cattle, sheep and goats, which mostly get their nourishment by eating grass.

▲ Wheat covers more of the world than any other crop.

Millions of people live on the world's open plains, growing wheat or maize on farms, or raising sheep or cattle on ranches. Farmers and ranchers sometimes look after immense areas of land. Grassland peoples include North America's cowboys, South America's cowboys (known as gauchos), Mongol horse herders of Central Asia, and Kenya's cattle-herding Masai.

▼ These horse herders live on the steppes of Mongolia, in Central Asia. They raise horses to sell, and regularly move with them to find fresh grazing land.

# Seas of Grass

There were once no grasses anywhere, because forests covered most of every continent. But after dinosaurs died out, around 65 million years ago, grasses slowly spread across lands that became too dry for trees.

## Temperate grasslands

There are two main types of grassland: temperate and tropical. Temperate grasslands lie north or south of the tropics. They are often in the middle of continents, or in the shadow of high mountains, where rainfall is low. The largest temperate grasslands in the world stretch from eastern Europe to China. Russians call these lands steppes, meaning grassy plains. Uzbek, Kirghiz, Kazakh and Mongolian people live there. On the Great Plain of Hungary, farmers grow wheat on a huge scale.

▼ The steppes in central Asia and the prairies in North America are the largest temperate grasslands. The largest tropical grasslands are the savannahs that lie across Africa.

## The world's grasslands

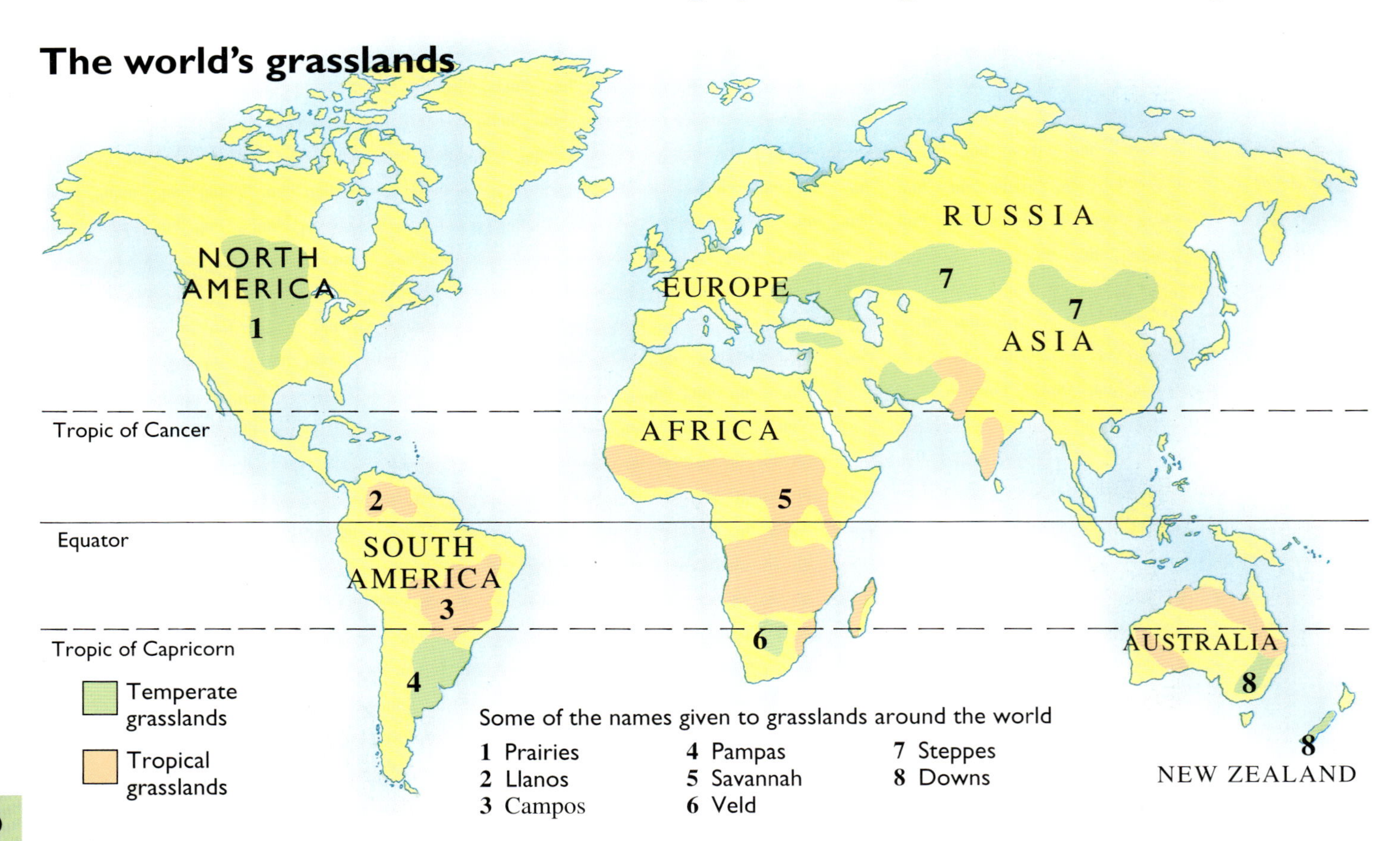

Another great sweep of temperate grassland, the prairies, sprawls across North America. Native American peoples who live there include the Blackfoot, Mandan and Sioux. Temperate grasslands have short grass and few trees. But most wild grassland in temperate regions has now been cleared for growing crops, or sown with cultivated grasses to provide grazing for farm animals.

## The Open Prairie

*An American traveller, Francis Parkman, crossed the prairies on horseback in the 1840s. He wrote: 'One day we rode for hours, without seeing a tree or a bush; before, behind, and on either side stretched the vast expanse... covered with the unbroken carpet of fresh green grass.'*

## Temperate grassland weather

Temperate grasslands can be very hot in summer and bitterly cold in winter. Most rain falls in the summer, when moist winds blow in from the sea. Winters are drier and there is often snow. Temperate grasslands are windy. In the prairies in spring and early summer, tall columns of whirling winds, called tornadoes, spin across the land, smashing homes and cars.

▼ A shepherd on horseback rounds up sheep with the help of sheepdogs, in the temperate downs of New Zealand.

## A temperate climate

Manitoba is a prairie province in Canada. Temperatures there can range from 32 °C in summer to –40 °C in winter. Most rain falls in the summer months.

## Tropical grasslands

Tropical grasslands, or savannahs, are also farmed and ranched, although vast stretches are still wild. Savannahs lie north and south of the tropical rain forests that grow around the Equator. The largest savannahs form a belt across Africa. Only clumps of grass and thorny bushes thrive in West Africa on the edge of the Sahara Desert, in the area called the Sahel. The Dogo, Bambara and Fulani people work the dry land there.

### Wildlife in Plenty

*In the early 1900s, a British nature expert called Cherry Kearton was amazed by the numbers of zebras and antelope she saw from a train crossing the Kenyan savannah: 'Thousands of animals of different species, either in big groups or dotted about the expanse... As the train rattled along... only a few of them moved away. No such sight could be seen anywhere else in the world.'*

In East Africa, most large wild animals are now found in reserves. Most of the land is used for growing crops such as maize and millet. East African peoples include the Masai and the Dinka, who are traditional herders.

▼ Kenya's wildebeest follow the rains in search of green pastures.

## Savannahs around the world

Several savannah regions lie in South America. Grassy plains, called llanos, cover much of Venezuela. The climate there is harsh, and the people who live on the llanos have a reputation for being tough and brave. South of the Amazon rain forest, wooded grasslands known as campos cover the hilly regions of Brazil. Brazil also has a flat savannah, called the pantanal.

Much of northern Australia and parts of India are tropical grasslands, with tough-leaved shrubs and few trees. Strange fat-trunked trees, called baobabs, grow on the Australian and African savannahs. One baobab tree trunk can hold up to 9,000 litres of water. Storing water helps baobabs live through months of drought.

### A savannah climate

Cloncurry is in Queensland, in north-east Australia. Here daily temperatures range from 38 °C in summer (the rainy season) to 24 °C in winter.

▲ A farmer in northern India uses cattle to pull a wooden plough, as Indian farmers have done for thousands of years.

## Savannah weather

Savannah days are warm or hot, but nights are cool or even chilly. For months the land stays dry. Then comes a rainy season lasting several weeks. In places, so much rain falls that floods occur. For a while, great stretches of the llanos and the pantanal vanish under water, and farmers have to move their cattle to higher ground.

# *History of Grassland People*

Two million years ago, the first-known humans lived on hot, East African grasslands. These early people made crude tools of stone and wood, so today they are known as *Homo habilis*, meaning handy people. They wandered the plains finding wild fruits and roots to eat and stealing meat from the carcases of grazing animals such as gazelles and wildebeest, killed by lions.

## Stone Age hunters

Before *Homo habilis* died out, a bigger, more intelligent type of human appeared in the African savannahs. *Homo erectus* (upright people) spread into Asia, and probably hunted with spears. From these humans came the first people like us, known as *Homo sapiens* (wise people). Our early ancestors were still hunter-gatherers. But they also made stone and bone weapons for killing big grazing mammals such as deer. *Homo sapiens* spread around the world. By 40,000 years ago they had reached Europe and Australia.

▼ Controlled bush fires, like this one, have been set alight by Australian Aborigines for thousands of years. They encourage fresh growth, which attracts animals to the area for the Aborigines to hunt.

This Stone-Age flint axe ▶
was used about 3,000 BC
by farmers in Europe to
chop down trees. The
wooden handle has been
added recently.

### Clearing the Forest

*In Denmark recently, a Stone - Age axe-head was put to the test. Three men chopped down more than 600 $m^2$ of beech forest in only four hours, using an axe fitted with the ancient head. Over 6,000 years ago, stone axes helped Stone-Age farmers to turn Europe's forests into fields.*

Around 100,0000 years ago, some early hunters began to change the natural world in which they lived, and helped to create grasslands. Stone-Age hunters, including Australian Aborigines, burnt down trees to make new pastures to attract the grazing animals they hunted. Later, in Europe and elsewhere, Stone-Age farmers began burning and chopping down forests to clear land to grow crops and create meadows for their sheep and cattle.

About 10,000 years ago, Native Americans were spearing buffaloes on the North American prairies. We know this because people have found their stone spearheads buried alongside old buffalo bones. Until 200 years ago, Australia's Aborigines and New Zealand's Maori also used Stone-Age weapons and hunted on foot.

## Taming the grasslands

Around 13,000 years ago, some grassland people stopped being hunters and became herders or shepherds. Instead of chasing wild beasts, they tamed them for food and for carrying loads. Cattle provided East African herders with milk, meat and hides. Later, shepherds and herders grazed sheep and goats across Asia's dry grasslands.

Around 4,500 years ago, groups of people wandered the steppes of Central Asia on horseback. Over the centuries, Huns and other warlike groups rode from these dry pastures, attacking Asian and European cities. Even in peacetime, shepherds and herders were often on the move, travelling to find fresh pastures for their animals to graze.

▼ A painting showing the Mongol leader Genghis Khan and his army in battle in 1201. Genghis Khan led fierce armies from the steppes of Central Asia to win an empire that stretched from the Black Sea to the Pacific Ocean.

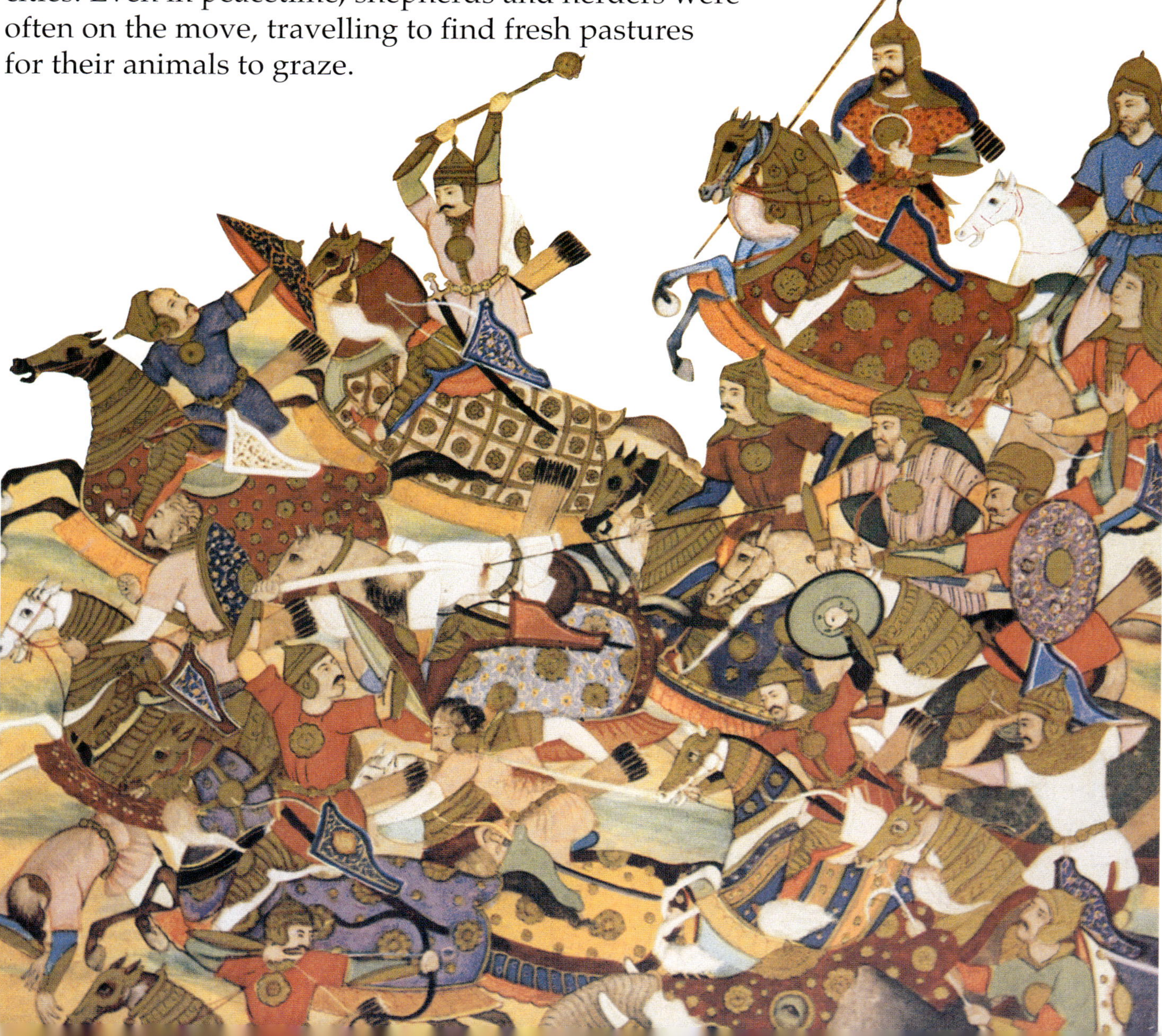

## Settling the grasslands

On wetter grasslands, people had begun to settle down and grow crops. By 7,000 years ago, Africans were sowing the savannah with millet and sorghum. In the Missouri Valley in North America, the Mandan people later grew beans, maize and squashes. They swapped spare food for other goods with wandering tribes.

▲ A painting of the Great Trek of the 1830s, when more than 12,000 Boer settlers trekked through South Africa to find fresh grazing grounds for their animals.

About 200 years ago, few people lived in the world's great grasslands. But Europe's population had grown fast, and Europeans wanted extra food and living space. By the mid-1800s, millions were emigrating to farm and ranch the pampas of South America, the North American prairies, the Asian steppes and the South African veld. From 1650, Dutch colonists, called Boers, settled the southern tip of Africa. In the 1830s, thousands of Boers began their Great Trek north, using ox-drawn wagons to search for new lands to farm. Many battles were fought as Europeans forced the local African peoples from their lands.

## History of Settlers

*Early 1800s:* Farmers begin to settle the American Midwest.
*1820s:* British sheep farmers settle the Australian downs.
*1836:* Boer farmers make their Great Trek through South Africa.
*1840s:* British settlers claim land in South Island, New Zealand.
*1850s:* Russian peasants settle the steppes of Kazakhstan, in Asia.

## Pioneer farmers

In the 1840s, pioneer farmers moved west across the North American Midwest. Cheap land and rich soil attracted people to these remote grasslands. But there were dangers. Droughts, blizzards and diseases struck the pioneers and their cattle as they crossed the prairies. The early homesteaders found little water, and their ploughs could not break through the tangled grass roots. Sheep and cattle invaded the crops they planted. Soon, new inventions helped life on the prairies. Windmills pumped up water from underground. Sharp steel ploughs were invented that could slice through tough soil, and barbed wire provided cheap fences to keep cattle out of crops.

▲ Pioneer families setting off across the American Midwest in the early 1800s, in wagons called prairie schooners. The schooners were pulled by mules or oxen, and up to 100 of them would form a long line called a wagon train.

The European settlers changed the way of life for Native Americans for ever. Before the Europeans arrived, groups such as the Blackfoot hunted buffaloes with spears and arrows. They hunted on foot, since there were no horses on the prairies at that time. The Europeans brought horses and guns to North America and by 1889, they had all but wiped out the buffalo.

Gradually, the settlers drove Native Americans from their lands and confined them to reservations. Native Americans fought many battles, but failed to win back their homelands. Many died of diseases such as cholera and smallpox, which were brought by the settlers.

## Hunting the Buffaloes

*Before Europeans arrived in North America, up to 70 million buffaloes roamed the prairies. Native Americans honoured the animal that provided them with meat. Buffalo hides were made into tents and clothes. But Europeans killed the buffaloes in great numbers, to clear the land for farming. By 1889, they had shot all but about 550 buffaloes.*

▲ Sioux warriors hunted buffaloes from horseback after Europeans introduced horses to North America.

▼ For thousands of years, Aborigines roamed the Australian Outback. When British settlers arrived in 1788 and fenced the land for farming, they destroyed the Aboriginal way of life.

By 1900, European farmers or ranchers were also developing grasslands in South America, Central Asia, East Africa, Australia and New Zealand. In hot grasslands, tropical diseases and pests attacked crops and cattle shipped from Europe. Large-scale farming did not take off in the African savannahs as it did on the American prairies, but ranching succeeded in South America, Australia and New Zealand. Ranchers developed new breeds of cattle that survived the heat, pests and diseases.

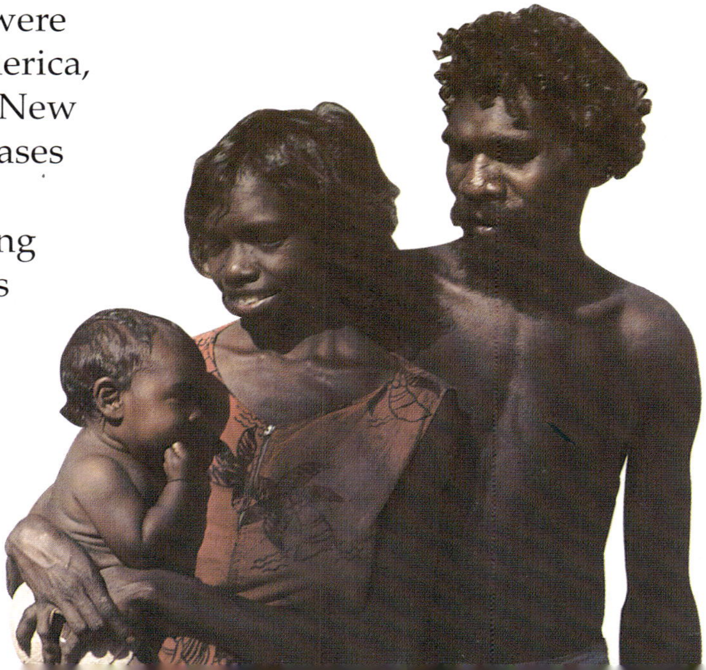

# Grassland Work

**Biggest grassland farms or ranches**

*Biggest cattle station:*
30,000 km$^2$
(Australia)
*Biggest sheep station:*
10,600 km$^2$
(New Zealand)
*Biggest arable farms:*
over 25,000 ha
(collective farms of the former Soviet Union)

Once covered with wild grasses, the vast spaces of the Asian steppes and North American prairies are among the world's most productive farmlands. Modern machines mean that a few people can now farm or ranch an immense stretch of land. One tractor pulling a plough with many blades can turn more soil in a day than a horse-drawn plough could do in weeks. Tractors speed the work of sowing, harrowing, spreading fertilizer and spraying pesticides. Sprinklers spray water on thirsty plants such as maize. Combine harvesters make quick work of gathering grain.

## Crops to sell, crops to eat

In wealthy countries, farmers mostly sell the crops they grow. These are called cash crops. Wheat, maize and potatoes are often cash crops. Farmers also grow plants for animals to eat, called fodder crops. Maize, rye grass and clover are fodder crops. One field might produce different crops in different years. This is called crop rotation, and helps to keep soil fertile.

▼ Aeroplanes spray pesticides on some of the world's largest fields. One pilot can spray a vast crop in less time than it would take a team of tractors.

In poorer countries, especially in dry, tropical grasslands, most people use hand tools and only grow enough food to eat. This is called subsistence farming. In Kenya, for instance, many Kikuyu people look after small plots of family land, growing crops such as millet and sorghum. Wetter, tropical grasslands produce cash crops, such as cotton, peanuts, sisal, tobacco and flowers.

▲ Zambian girls pound grain into flour, collect it in baskets and sieve out dirt and stones. The flour is used for making porridge or bread.

## Ranching

Different types of animals thrive on different types of land. Goats can eat scrawny plants. Sheep can manage on poorer grassland than cattle. Dairy cattle (kept mainly for milk) do best in mild, wet climates. Beef cattle thrive there, too, but also in the tropics.

The number of animals a piece of land can support depends on how much food they find there. It takes a lot of poor grassland to feed one cow or sheep. In the Kimberley region of Australia, one cattle station is nearly as big as Belgium, and one Australian sheep fence is as long as the North Atlantic Ocean is wide.

## Herding

In mountain grasslands, herders and shepherds drive their animals to new pastures according to the seasons. In Central Asia and Europe, shepherds drive flocks of sheep uphill in spring to feed on fresh mountain pastures. In autumn, they lead them downhill to escape the winter cold. In dry African grasslands close to the Sahara Desert, flocks and herds are moved according to the seasons. New grass provides good grazing after rain.

**Keeping Dingoes Out**

***Australia's 5,300-kilometre-long Dingo Fence protects south-east Australia's sheep from dingoes. Dingoes are wild dogs that roam the rest of the country. However, storms and kangaroos can punch holes in the wire mesh. So finding and mending holes is full-time work for fence patrols.***

▼ Vaqueiros (cowboys) rounding up cattle on a ranch in Saõ Paulo, Brazil.

On the savannah of West Africa, the Fulani are nomadic cattle herders. They travel long distances to find fresh pastures for their cattle, and take care to move on before their animals overgraze the land. Sometimes even small children are put in charge of a large herd.

▲ A Masai boy looks after his hump-backed cattle as they graze on wild grassland in Tanzania.

## Farms make work

Crops and livestock provide work for other people besides farmers and ranchers. Salespeople persuade farmers to buy fertilizers, pesticides and farm machinery, to make farm work easier. Lorry drivers take cattle, grain and other products to market. Dealers buy and sell these goods at auctions. Other people work at flour mills, bakeries, dairies and abattoirs, turning crops and animals into bread, cheese, meat and other products. This food processing goes on largely in towns or cities on the grasslands. But farm machinery, pesticides and fertilizers are often manufactured far away.

### Top producers of grassland products

| | |
|---|---|
| Barley | *Russia* |
| Beef | *USA* |
| Horses | *China* |
| Maize | *USA* |
| Oats | *Russia* |
| Rice | *China* |
| Sheep | *Australia* |
| Sugar-cane | *Brazil* |
| Sunflower seed | *Argentina* |
| Wheat | *China* |

In local towns and cities, many jobs depend upon farmers and their families. Townspeople work in shops, offices, schools and hospitals to supply families with everything from education to medicine.

▲ Ranchers inspect sheep for sale at an auction in New South Wales, Australia. Livestock auctions attract buyers from hundreds of kilometres away.

## Mining the grasslands

Not all grassland towns depend on farming. Some are mining communities. Thousands of wells produce oil and gas in Wyoming, a prairie and mountain state in the USA. Black Thunder Mine in Wyoming is the biggest coal mine in North and South America. From its open pits, giant draglines armed with scoops the size of swimming pools claw out a tonne of coal a second, and drop it in colossal dumper trucks. Oil has also been discovered in the llanos of Venezuela. It is pumped by pipeline to refineries on the Caribbean coast.

◀ Many of the men who mine South Africa's gold have left their homes far away to work thousands of metres below ground.

▼ A Soviet space rocket blasts off into space from the cosmodrome at Baykonur, in Kazakhstan.

Huge supplies of iron and diamonds come from open-cast mines in dry grasslands of north-west Australia, and more than half the world's gold comes from South African grasslands. The deepest mines are very hot and airless, and artificially cooled air has to be pumped in for miners. Rockfalls are another danger, because of the great weight of rock pressing down on tunnels.

## Testing ground

From the late 1950s, the deserted grasslands of Kazakhstan, in Central Asia, were used by the USSR for scientific tests of various kinds. With few people living there, it was easy to keep their discoveries secret. The first satellite, called Sputnik, and the first man and woman were launched into space from Baykonur, on the steppe east of the Aral Sea. Unfortunately, the Soviets also used the steppes as a testing ground for nuclear weapons. From 1949–89, about 470 nuclear bombs were exploded near Semey. The damage caused to the environment and to local people is still felt today.

# Transport and Communications

Modern roads and railways mean that crops grown on the grasslands supply food for millions of people living around the world.

## The coming of railways

Steam-powered rail locomotives provided the first way of transporting large amounts of goods quickly over the North American prairies. In the 1860s, two companies began building the first railway to cross North America. First, teams of workers marked out the route, driving Native Americans from the land. Then came construction gangs, followed by track-laying crews. Teams of labourers worked inland from the west and east coasts, and met up in Utah, in 1869. More railways quickly pushed into the prairies. Ranchers were soon driving cattle hundreds of kilometres to their nearest railway station, to be transported to the eastern cities.

▼ Trains still provide a quick, cheap way of moving goods across the North American prairies. Most long-distance travellers now go by air, which is faster still.

The railways of North America are now over 100 years old. People can no longer take a train on the great Canadian-Pacific Railroad, but the line is still used to carry grain and minerals from the grasslands.

In the nineteenth century, the British controlled Kenya in East Africa. They built railways to link savannah areas to ports such as Mombasa. Building the railway lines was difficult and often dangerous. Lions dragged several construction workers from their tents at night and killed them.

By 1900, railways were also opening up the great plains of Russia, Argentina and Uruguay. The Trans-Siberian Railway was built over 100 years ago to link Moscow and Beijing across the vast steppes of Central Asia. Passengers can still travel on this route, which is the longest railway journey in the world, lasting nine-and-a-half days.

▲ The Trans-Siberian Express halts at a station in central Russia, on the longest railway journey in the world.

**Pony Express**

*The fastest way to send messages across the North American prairies was once by Pony Express. In 1860, relays of horse riders took ten days to gallop more than 3,000 km from Missouri to California. But in 1861, telegraph operators began flashing messages instantly by wire, and the Pony Express went out of business.*

◀ This painting shows the first Pony Express rider leaving Missouri, USA, in 1860.

## Roads through the plains

Since 1900, broad, hard-surfaced roads have linked prairie towns and cities. Trucks and buses using these routes now carry much of the traffic that once went by train. In Australia, trucks pulling several trailers, called road trains, carry livestock and grain through the outback. In Venezuela, lorries carry grain and timber more than a thousand kilometres along the busy highway that crosses the upper plains. Along the Pan-American Highway, traffic also speeds through the grasslands of Uruguay and Brazil.

▲ Sixty-two wheels speed this 50-metre road train's string of petrol tanks through Australia's Northern Territory.

▼ A crop is carried on an ox-cart in Salvador, Central America. Many loads in Central and South America are still transported in this way.

Off the main roads, dirt tracks lead to remote farms and ranches. In Paraguay, many main roads are still mud, with deep holes and ruts dug out by shabby old lorries and buses. Here, ox-carts still bring cotton to market.

## Boats and ships

Riverboats and ocean-going ships also carry grain and livestock from grasslands to market. In the USA, huge barges take grain down the Mississippi river to the Gulf of Mexico, to be shipped all over the world. From coastal ports, ships carry beef from Brazil and Argentina, and lamb from New Zealand to places as far off as North America and Europe. This long-distance meat trade began in 1877, when the first cargo of frozen meat sailed from Argentina to France. Freezing stopped the meat from going bad.

▼ Tugboats push or pull whole groups of barges, known as tows, along the Mississippi river.

Great rivers also cut through the Asian steppes, but most flow northwards, in the wrong direction to carry grain from the wheat-growing lands. In Australia, the Murray-Darling river stretches 3,700 km from the Snowy Mountains to near Adelaide. Small boats use the river, but parts are too shallow for larger ones.

## Aeroplanes and helicopters

Where distances are huge, aeroplanes are used to help ranch sheep and cattle. In northern Australia, herds roam cattle stations nearly as big as small countries. Once a year, the station owners round up all the cattle they can catch. Horse-riders used to take part in this muster. Now it is often done by helicopter.

Aeroplanes help people to travel quickly where good roads are scarce. Many Venezuelan and Australian ranchers fly small private planes to towns instead of driving there by truck. In Australia and some other countries, small planes also take doctors to visit sick or injured people in remote places, or bring patients to hospital.

> **Flying Doctors**
>
> ***John Holmes is a flying doctor based in Derby, Western Australia. He reports: 'Pilots fly doctors and nurses out to emergencies in the outback. We rush very ill people to hospital. But much of our work is routine. We hold clinics in remote towns and villages, and patients come to see us there just as anyone might visit their local doctor.'***

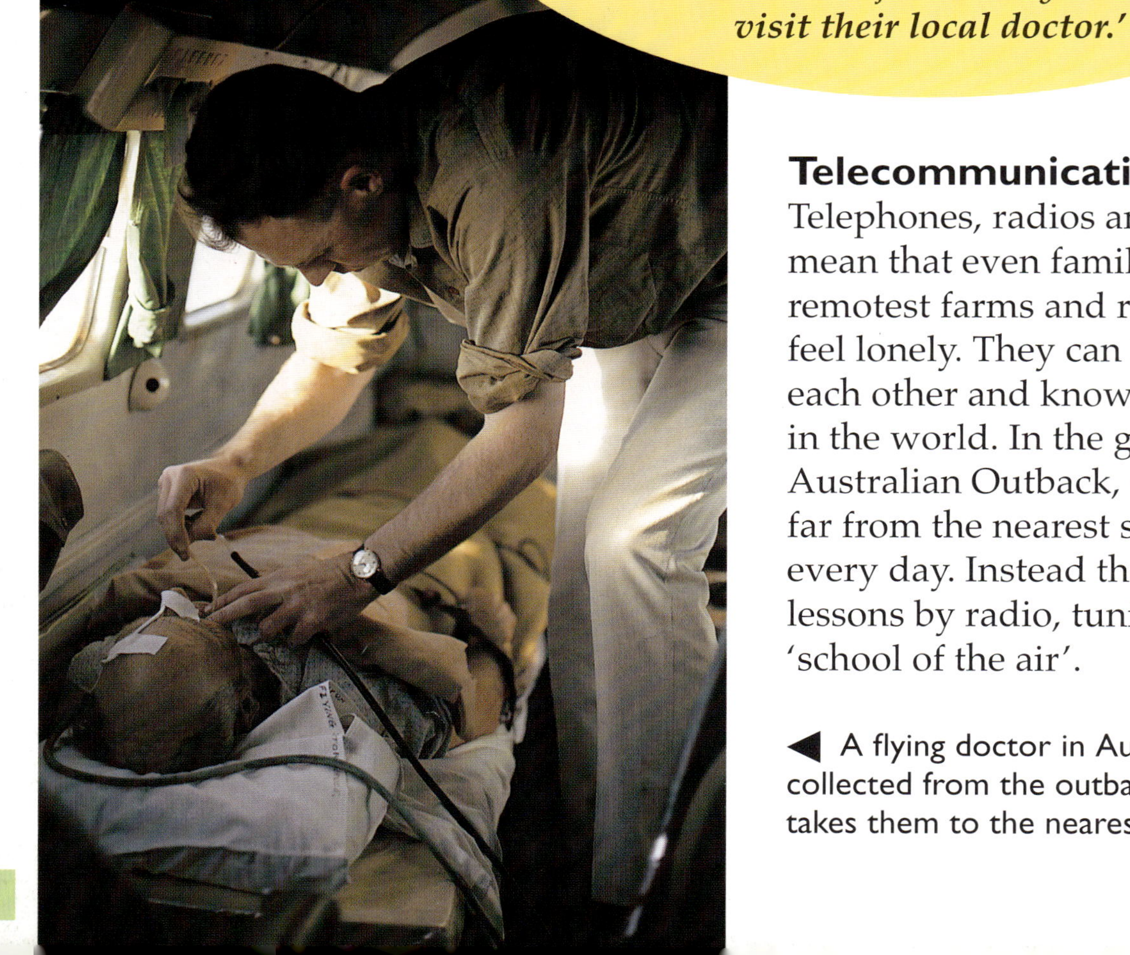

## Telecommunications

Telephones, radios and televisions mean that even families on the remotest farms and ranches need never feel lonely. They can keep in touch with each other and know what is going on in the world. In the grasslands of the Australian Outback, children live too far from the nearest school to go there every day. Instead they learn their lessons by radio, tuning in to the 'school of the air'.

◀ A flying doctor in Australia treats a patient collected from the outback, as the aeroplane takes them to the nearest hospital.

▼ A helicopter rounds up cattle in Australia.

# Homes and Buildings

The first grassland homes were simple shelters to protect families from rain, wind, sunshine and cold. People built using whatever materials were handy.

## Movable homes

Native Americans of the prairies lived near rivers at first, in villages of earth-covered houses called lodges. Each lodge sheltered several families. In summer, the women stayed at home and tended crops, while the men went off to hunt for buffalo and deer. After 1600, when horses were introduced by the Spaniards, Native Americans followed the grazing buffalo herds all year round. Whole families lived in tall, pointed tents called tipis. A tipi had a frame of poles covered in buffalo hides. Open flaps at the top allowed smoke to escape from the campfire inside.

▼ A group of Comanche Native American women outside their tipi, which is made of buffalo skins. The photograph was taken in present-day Oklahoma, USA, in about 1870.

▲ A Chinese family in northern China, outside their yurt.

In other grassland areas, nomadic peoples travelling with their herds still live in lightweight, movable homes. In Central Asia, Mongol herders make a framework of poles with upright walls and a low, domed roof, covered with windproof woollen felt. These homes are called yurts. On the cold, high plateau of Tibet, shepherds spend most of the year in tents of woven yak hair.

Tents, yurts and tipis are easy to put up and take down. Once dismantled, people load them on to horses, camels or yaks, to be carried to a new pasture. There, the nomads can quickly set up home again.

▲ Wealthy Mongols live in large, comfortably furnished yurts like this one, which are often set up permanently in towns.

## Settled homes

On North America's prairies, the white settlers found no wood to build with. Instead, these pioneer farmers chopped strips of ploughed earth into blocks, and stacked them up like bricks to build walls. Then they added a roof made of thatch. The floor was bare clay. These small, crumbly homes were called sod houses.

Where trees grew at the prairie edge, cattle farmers built long, log-cabin ranch houses. There would also be a cookhouse, and a bunkhouse for the cowboys to sleep in.

▼ A sod house with earth walls and an earth-covered roof still stands in the Oglala National Grasslands, in Nebraska, USA.

▲ Masai herdsmen in Kenya sit outside a traditional dung-covered hut.

In East Africa, Masai cattle herders lived in villages of long, low huts made of branches and brushwood, plastered with mud and cow dung. Skin roofs kept out the rain. The huts formed a large circle, surrounded by a tall, thorn fence. Villagers drive their cattle inside the fence at night to keep them safe from lions.

## Homes old and new

In Central Asia, nomadic Mongols still live in yurts, and Tibetan shepherds spend summer in tents. In East Africa, some Masai still live in huts made of mud and dung. However, farms have now taken over much of the Masai's old pastureland, and many have been forced to move on, or to grow crops. Today, many Masai live in shacks, with walls made of concrete blocks or wooden planks, and roofs of corrugated iron.

When trains and trucks brought timber into the treeless steppes and prairies, people started to build with wood. Wooden houses sprang up on the prairies. Today, most Tibetan shepherds spend the bitter winters in snug, wooden homes.

**Timber House**

*Jigme, a shepherd from the high Tibetan plateau, says: 'No trees grow up here, but when the road came, trucks brought in big wooden posts. That's how we were able to build our winter home. It's much warmer than living in a tent. The winters up here are bitterly cold.'*

Today, smartly painted wooden houses stand dotted about the downs of Australia and the North American plains. Older Australian farmhouses have wooden walls and a wide porch, while more modern homes have walls of brick.

Most North American farmhouses are still timber-built. The powerful winds of a tornado can blow down even a strong wooden house, so prairie houses often have storm cellars. When the radio gives a storm warning, the whole family goes down into the storm cellar and stays there until the howling winds and driving rain have passed. Modern farmhouses have electricity and many are air-conditioned to keep them cool in the scorching summer weather.

▲ Farm buildings in Kansas, USA, shelter livestock, machinery and harvested crops.

▼ A tornado spins across a wheat field in the American prairies.

▲ The main street of Wyroff, Minnesota, a prairie town in the American Midwest. Prairie towns often have several stores and bars, a pool hall, bank and a post office.

## Wide Open Spaces

***If you fly across the prairies, pampas or Australian downs, you can see that each set of buildings stands among its own fields. Since so many farms are vast, farmhouses are often far apart. An hour's drive or more can separate the buildings of one Australian cattle station from those of the next! The nearest town may be 100 km away.***

## Grassland towns

On the world's great grasslands, towns are mostly small. They have just enough shops and other businesses to meet the everyday needs of the surrounding farms. In the Australian Outback, small, dusty towns usually have one wide street, one store, two or three bars and little else. Similar small towns stand here and there across the Argentinian pampas.

# Leisure and Tourism

Grasslands used to be places where only country people lived and worked. Nowadays, many city people also go there to enjoy their leisure time.

## Traditional leisure

Before machines arrived, farmers and ranchers had little leisure time. On the North American prairies, cowhands and farmers usually worked from dawn till dark. In their time off, some took part in lassoing or bucking bronco competitions.

Nowadays, people living in the grasslands enjoy modern sports such as football, baseball, golf and racing. But traditional fairs, festivals, cattle shows and sports contests also play an important part in their lives. They are also attractions for tourists, who come from far away to watch.

▼ A gaucho (cowboy) in Argentina taking part in the November Festival of Tradition, in San Antonio de Areco. This festival celebrates the traditional life of the gauchos.

▼ A cowboy is thrown from his horse in the Pendleton Rodeo, USA.

**Rodeo**

*Every July, about a million tourists flock to the Exhibition and Stampede rodeo at Calgary, in Canada, which lasts for ten days. One of its most exciting events is a chuck-wagon race, where teams of galloping horses haul wagons around a track.*

◀ A game of polo in Argentina. Polo began in Iran, but it is now a popular sport in many parts of the world.

## Fairs and festivals

Traditional fairs and festivals are special occasions when people come together to have fun at certain times of the year. Families from a wide area often travel to fairs. People try their hands at sporting competitions, or gather round to watch.

On the Asian steppes, Mongolian herders gather at fairs to sell their horses. There are horse races, and archery and wrestling contests. In New Zealand and Australia, popular contests include sheep-shearing, with prizes for the ranch-hands who can shear the most sheep in a given time.

The fastest Australian and ▶ New Zealand sheep-shearers can shear the wool off more than eighty sheep per hour.

▲ Young riders race to the finish at the Naadam Festival in Mongolia. The race is part of a traditional festival, held each year near Ulan Bator, Mongolia's capital.

### Young Champions

***On the steppes of Central Asia, children of herders learn to ride as soon as they can walk. At the annual Naadam Festival in Mongolia, one of the most important horse races is for child riders under the age of ten. The prize for the winner is 100 stallions.***

## Tourism

Nowadays, city people also stay on farms and ranches to learn what life is like in the world's grasslands. Many Australian farms take paying guests. On the Argentinian pampas you can stay on one of the huge ranches, called *estancias,* and go riding and play polo. On the llanos of Venezuela you can even take part in a wild-horse round-up. North American ranches that take holiday-makers teach riding, lassoing and other traditional cowboy skills.

In northern China, guided tours take visitors to the remote grasslands of Inner Mongolia to watch expert Mongol riders giving displays on camels and horses. In the evening there may be a banquet with a whole roasted sheep. Local people sing and dance. Tourists can also hire jeeps, and drive out into the lonely plains. They stay in guest yurts, much smarter than the mud-floored homes that Mongolian nomads live in.

▲ Tourists photograph a young African elephant in a national park in Kenya. Kenya earns a lot of money from foreign visitors, who pay to go on safari to see its wildlife.

## Wildlife holidays

Most visitors to the world's tropical grasslands go to see the wildlife. Once, only a few hunters from Europe and North America went went on safari to shoot big game on foot. Now, minibuses take thousands of tourists armed with cameras on safari through East Africa. In an open-roofed minibus, you can get close enough to film or photograph lions, elephants, giraffes and zebras. Very wealthy tourists can ride in a hot-air balloon to see the wildlife from above.

## Wildlife Watch

***Visitors to the Venezuelan llanos can see more types of wildlife than anywhere outside a zoo, especially on ranches where wildlife is protected. On one ranch, people have spotted over fifty types of mammals and over 300 types of birds.***

Wildlife also draws tourists to the llanos of Venezuela, in South America. Parts of the llanos teem with wild birds and mammals. In northern Australia, tourists can take trips around the 20,000 $km^2$ Kakadu National Park, where they can see parrots, kangaroos and crocodiles.

▲ Two capybaras in the llanos of Venezuela. Capybaras are the world's largest rodent.

▼ These Masai girls are wearing their traditional costume as a show for tourists.

# The Future

▲ Genetic engineers study new types of plants at the Institute of Tropical Agriculture in Nigeria.

Grasslands have always been the 'breadbaskets' of the world. But as human populations grow, farmers and ranchers will need to squeeze even more food from these vast, flat lands. They may try to produce extra food in two ways: by making farms and ranches yield bigger crops, and by using extra land.

## Genetic engineering

To squeeze extra food from the land, farmers now use new types of cereal plants which produce bigger crops and are also resistant to disease. New types of wheat and rice help India's farmers produce much bigger crops than in the 1950s. But to produce larger crops, farmers must buy extra fertilizer. Genetic engineering may help to save them money. By taking live ingredients from tiny germs and putting them in living plants, scientists are trying to invent a type of wheat that produces its own nitrate fertilizer. Genetic engineering like this already helps some types of crops to resist the pests that damage them or cause disease.

A prairie farmer checks ▶ his wheat to see if the crop is ready for harvesting.

## Creating more farmland

Finding extra farmland is difficult, and often causes damage. People already farm almost all the grassland suitable for crops or livestock. Most of the remaining wild grasslands are on the edges of deserts, or in nature reserves. Sheep and goats herded on the edge of the Sahara Desert kill the trees and plants by eating their leaves. This leaves the thin soil bare and at risk of being blown away by winds. If rain does not come, these areas can change from grasslands into desert.

In western Brazil, ranchers burn down tropical rainforest to create new pastures. But the poor soil beneath the trees is quickly washed away by heavy rain. Within ten years, these areas cannot produce enough grass for the cattle, so the ranchers clear more forest. This upsets the climate of the area. Over time, the climate becomes drier, and the soil bakes hard, making it very difficult for the rainforest to grow again.

▼ A shepherd's flock finds few plants to nibble in the Sahel in Senegal. To feed fast-growing human populations, African shepherds use even the scantiest pastures.

A rhinoceros shading from ▶ the midday sun in Kenya. Between the late 1970s and early 1990s, the numbers of black rhinoceroses in Africa fell from 30,000 to 3,500. Now they are protected in wildlife reserves.

## Wildlife threats

When wild grasslands are turned into farmland, wildlife can disappear. In Africa, some of the world's last large wild grasslands have become nature reserves. But farmland borders the reserves, and sometimes farmers and herdsmen go in to hunt the elephants that trample their crops and the lions that maul their cattle.

## People threats

When farmers plough up steppes and savannahs, local people often suffer. In the 1950s, when Russian and Ukrainian farmers fenced off the steppes of Kazakhstan, wandering herders and shepherds lost their grazing lands. This is happening today to the Masai cattle herders of Kenya. Herders and shepherds who lose their lands may be forced to settle down and farm.

▼ These Masai cattle herders may lose their grazing land to nature reserves or big farms. Many Masai now raise crops on small farms.

The use of machinery in farming and the closure of mines threaten towns in some grassland areas. Small towns are dying on the North American prairies. As mines close and machines take over work once done by farmhands, miners and farmhands lose their jobs and move away to find work in the cities. So small-town shops lose trade and close down for good.

**Lost Town**

*'I'm Mary Pyke. My family lived in Lost Springs, Wyoming. It was a busy little town – a railhead where cowboys brought their cattle. But when ranchers began to truck their cattle straight to market, trade fell off. Stores closed and people moved away. Lost Springs once held 5,000 people. Now there are just five.'*

## Exhausting the soil

Trying to squeeze extra food from grasslands can have the opposite effect. When herders let too many sheep or cattle graze a piece of land, the soil produces less food, not more. The same thing happens if farmers do not put back the nourishment their crops have taken from the soil. Then the soil becomes loose enough for wind and rain to blow or wash it away. Crops cannot grow where soil has been eroded. In the 1930s, on the North American prairies, years of drought turned the topsoil into powder. Fierce winds carried away loose soil in great dark clouds that hid the sun for days. Farmers were forced to leave their lands, and the problem became so bad that much of the Midwest was nicknamed the 'Dust Bowl'.

▼ Two farming families in the American Midwest leaving their farms in 1937, in the 'Dust Bowl' period.

## Solving the problems

Most of these problems have solutions. Practising crop rotation helps to nourish the soil. By growing a number of different crops, farmers cut down the risk of losing all their harvest to disease. In special centres, scientists store seeds of traditional crops in case disease wipes out those grown today. Local people can also help improve dry grasslands. In Burkina Faso, south of the Sahara Desert, farmers built low walls of stones across their fields to hold back irrigated soil. The year after the walls were finished, crop harvests doubled.

## Organic farming

One solution to the problem of soil exhaustion is organic farming, which uses animal manure and plant compost instead of chemical fertilizers. Organic farmers control insect pests through crop rotation, and by introducing other insects that eat the pests, instead of chemical pesticides. Many practise mixed farming (raising livestock as well as growing crops), which helps keep soil healthy. Although organic farms use more workers, farmers save money they would have spent on chemicals. Organic farming is becoming more popular in grassland areas worldwide, as more people demand organic vegetables, fruit and meat that are grown naturally and are thought to be more healthy.

▼ Kikuyu women in Kenya preparing plant compost. The women will use the compost instead of artificial fertilizer.

## Restoring the Land

***Strip mining once scarred Wyoming USA with deep open pits. New laws make mining companies restore the land when they have finished with it. Earth-moving machines fill in the pits and smooth the topsoil. Then people put back the kinds of plants that used to grow there.***

While food producers make the most of farms and ranches, governments and conservation groups try to save the last wild grasslands and their creatures. Governments compensate local people forced out of nature reserves, or driven off their land by farming.

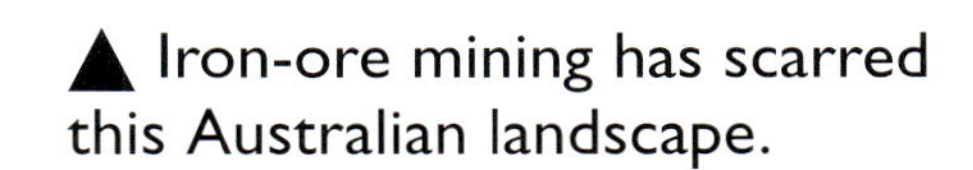

▲ Iron-ore mining has scarred this Australian landscape.

In Africa, many elephants have been killed by poachers who sell the tusks as ivory. African governments have made the trade illegal, and armed guards now patrol nature reserves to keep the poachers out. In Kenya's national parks, money earned from tourism adds to local people's income. This encourages them to help save the savannah and its wildlife too.

Kenyan officials making a bonfire of elephant tusks seized from poachers in 1991. ▶

# Glossary

**Aborigines** People who first lived in a place. This word is also used to refer to the original inhabitants of Australia.

**Bucking broncos** Half-wild horses that rear and plunge to shake off their riders.

**Campos** Hilly tropical grasslands in Brazil.

**Cash crop** A crop grown to be sold.

**Cattle station** An Australian ranch.

**Cereals** Foods made from the plump seeds of wheat or other grasses.

**Crop rotation** Growing a different crop on the same land each year.

**Downs** Rolling treeless uplands in Australia, New Zealand and England.

**Dust Bowl** Farmland where drought and wind turn soil to dust and crops die.

**Fertilizer** Any substance added to soil to nourish plants.

**Flying doctor** A doctor who visits patients by plane, especially in remote parts of Australia.

**Food processing** Turning plant or animal substances into foods such as bread, cheese and canned meat.

**Gauchos** South American cowboys.

**Genetic engineering** Producing new types of plants or animals by changing one or more of the genes that parent plants or animals pass on to their young.

**Llanos** Tropical grasslands of northern South America.

**Midwest** The northern-central part of the USA.

**Nomads** People who regularly wander from place to place to find food or water, for themselves or for their animals.

**Organic farming** Farming without the use of artificial fertilizers or pesticides.

**Pampas** Temperate grasslands in South America.

**Pantanal** Tropical grassland with trees in south-west Brazil.

**Pesticide** A substance used to kill pests or weeds.

**Ranch** A farm for breeding livestock, especially cattle.

**Range** Open countryside.

**Ranger** Someone who looks after a park or nature reserve.

**Rodeo** A show where people rope cattle or perform other cowboy skills.

**Safari** A journey through wild tropical countryside.

**Savannah** Tropical grassland, often with scattered bushes and trees.

**Sod** A slab of earth dug up by a spade or turned over by a plough.

**Subsistence farming** Growing crops to be eaten by the people who grow them.

**Veld** Grassland and dry open land in South Africa.

**Yurt** A felt-covered tent.

# Further Information

## Books to read

*Animals by Habitat: Animals of the Grasslands* by Steven Savage (Wayland, 1996)

*BBC Wildlife* and *National Geographic* magazines often have interesting articles on grasslands and grassland peoples.

*First Starts: Feeding the World* by Janine Amos (Watts, 1996)

*Habitats: Grasslands* by Julia Waterlow (Wayland, 1996)

*Jump Ecology: Life in the Plains* by Catherine Bradley (Watts, 1991)

*The Australian Outback and its People* by Kate Darian-Smith and David Lowe (Wayland, 1994)

*The Prairies and their People* by David Flint (Wayland, 1993)

*Ways of Life: Farming Communities* by Brian Williams (Cherrytree, 1992)

*What Do We Know About: The Plains Indians* by Dr. Colin Taylor (Macdonald Young Books, 1993)

**CD Roms**
*Exploring Land Habitats* (Wayland, 1997)

## Useful addresses

The following organisations can provide pamphlets and educational material for schools on grassland habitats around the world:

Friends of the Earth (UK),
26–28 Underwood Street, London N1 7JQ
Tel: 0171 490 1555

Greenpeace, Canonbury Villas, London N1 2PN Tel: 0171 865 8100

Intermediate Technology Development Group, Myson House, Railway Terrace, Rugby, Warwickshire CV21 3BR

Ministry of Agriculture, Fisheries & Food have produced a free booklet all about organic farming, called *Food Sense*..
Tel: 0645 556000

Worldwide Fund for Nature, Panda House, Weyside Park, Godalming, Surrey GU7 1XR
Tel: 01483 426444

**Picture acknowledgements**
The publisher would like to thank the following for allowing their pictures to be used in this book:
Bruce Coleman 39 (top); Corbis Bettmann 43; Eye Ubiquitous 22, 25, 30; Image Bank 26, 40 (lower), 32 (lower), 33; Impact Photos 1, 29 (top), 19, 32 (top), 34, 42 (top), 45 (lower); Museum of London 11; Novosti Press Agency 21 (lower); Peter Newark Pictures 12, 13, 14, 15 (top), 23 (lower); Panos Pictures 10, 15 (lower), 45 (top), 21 (top), 23 (top), 24 (top), 24 (lower), 29 (lower), 31, 37, 40 (top), 41, 42 (lower), 44; Pictor International 16; Taylor Archives 28; Tony Stone Worldwide *Chapter openers*, 2–3, 4, 5 (top), 5 (lower), 7, 8, 9, 17, 35, 36 (lower), 38, 39 (top); Wayland Picture Library *Cover*, 18 , 36 (top); Zefa Picture Library 20.

# Index

Page numbers in **bold** refer to photographs.